Smithsonian

HOW TO DRAW
AMAZING ANIMALS

WRITTEN BY KRISTEN MCCURRY
ILLUSTRATED BY LEONARDO MESCHINI

CAPSTONE PRESS
a capstone imprint

TABLE OF CONTENTS

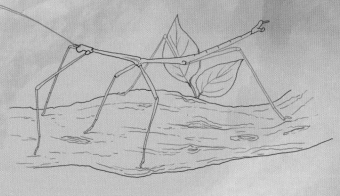

STEP 1

STEP 2

STEP 3

Weighing in at up to 11 tons (10 metric tons), the African elephant is the largest land animal on Earth. Its long trunk has more than 10,000 muscles. The elephant uses its trunk to breathe, smell, drink, make trumpeting sounds, and grab things. To help with that are two small fingerlike extensions at the end of the trunk.

STEP 4

FINISHED!

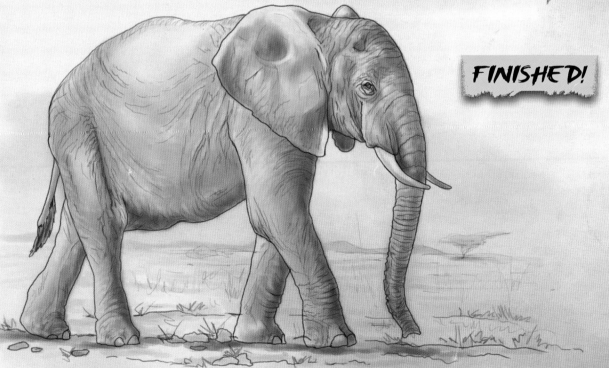

ALLIGATOR

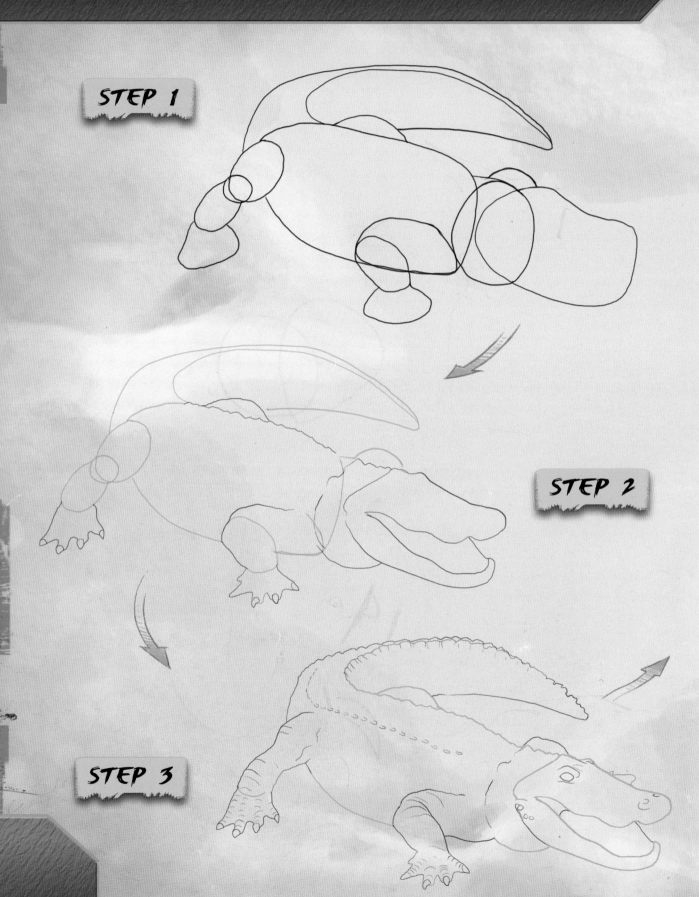

STEP 1

STEP 2

STEP 3

Unlike dinosaurs, this ancient species has managed to survive for millions of years. Alligators will eat nearly anything that crosses their path. They swallow small prey whole. Alligator eggs don't start as male or female—the temperature of each nest determines whether the hatchlings in it will be male or female.

STEP 4

FINISHED!

ARABIAN HORSE

STEP 1

STEP 2

STEP 3

The Arabian is the oldest known breed of riding horse, developed in Arabia before the seventh century. It is believed that Genghis Khan, Napoleon, and George Washington all rode Arabians. These horses are about 15 "hands" high at the withers (shoulders). That equals about 5 feet (1.5 meters).

STEP 4

FINISHED!

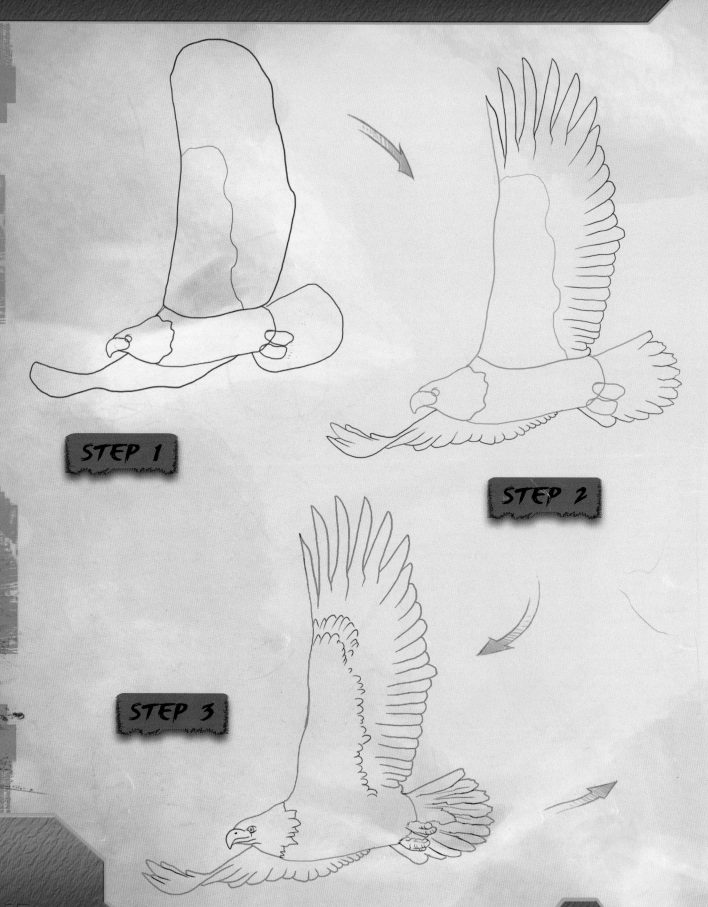

STEP 1

STEP 2

STEP 3

This national symbol of the United States was once nearly extinct, but its numbers are growing again. With sharp beaks and talons, bald eagles hunt fish and small animals. They will even steal prey other animals have caught. With their wingspan of about 6½ feet (2 m), these raptors can be spotted throughout North America.

STEP 4

FINISHED!

BARN OWL

The barn owl is one of the most widespread of all land birds. It has a white, heart-shaped face and is sometimes called the monkey-faced owl. It has small eyes for an owl, but is still good a hunter of small rodents. Barn owls have been known to nest in barn lofts, which is how they got their name.

STEP 4

FINISHED!

BASILISK LIZARD

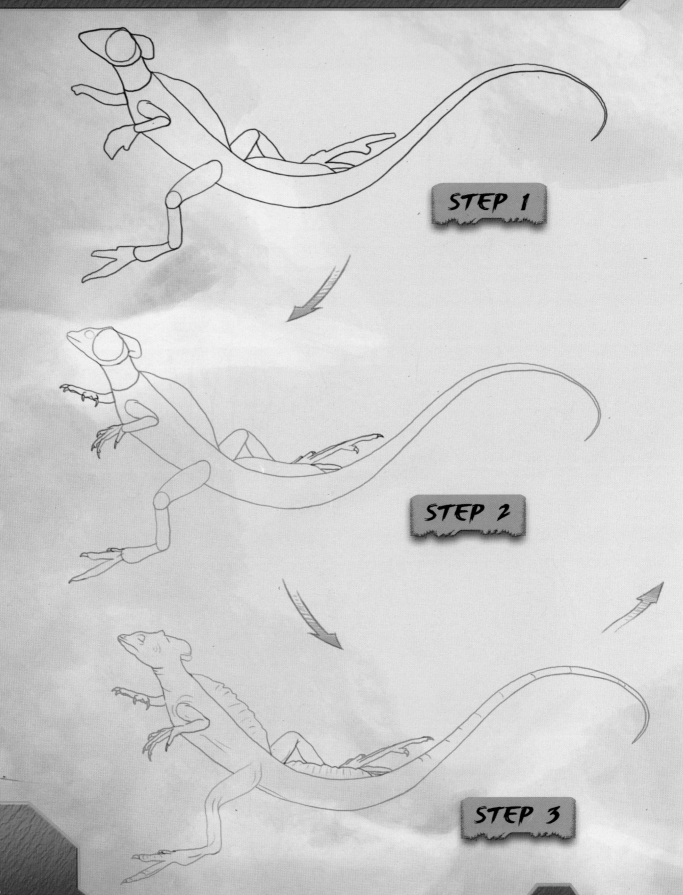

STEP 1

STEP 2

STEP 3

This medium-sized green lizard's claim to fame is its ability to walk—or run—on water when frightened. Special fringes of skin between its long toes spread out on top of the water as the lizard zips along at a speed of 5 feet (1.5 m) per second. It can keep this up for 15 feet (4.6 m) or so and then swims the rest of the way to its destination.

STEP 4

FINISHED!

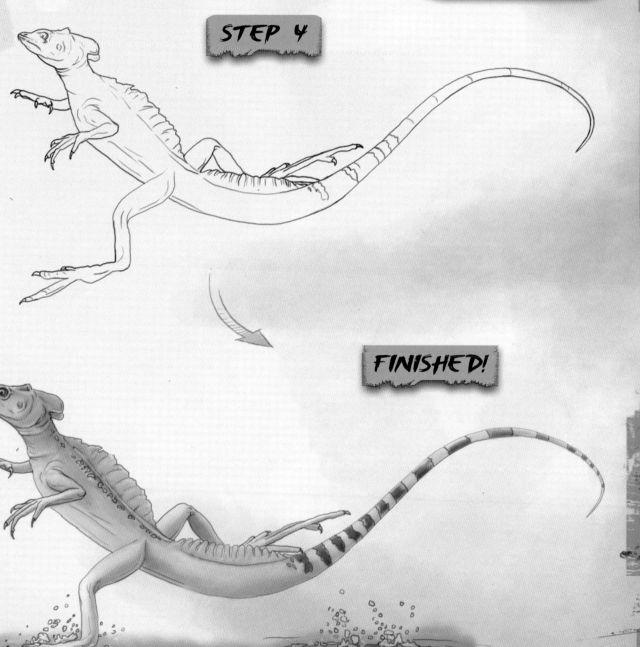

BLACK RHINOCEROS

STEP 1

STEP 2

STEP 3

This two-horned rhinoceros from Africa is also known as a hook-lipped rhino, which describes the pointy feature on its top lip. Its large front horn may be as long as 3½ feet (1 m). The rhino uses this horn to defend itself and to tear out bushes or even trees. After this fierce display, the plant-eating rhino eats the leaves and twigs.

STEP 4

FINISHED!

CHEETAH

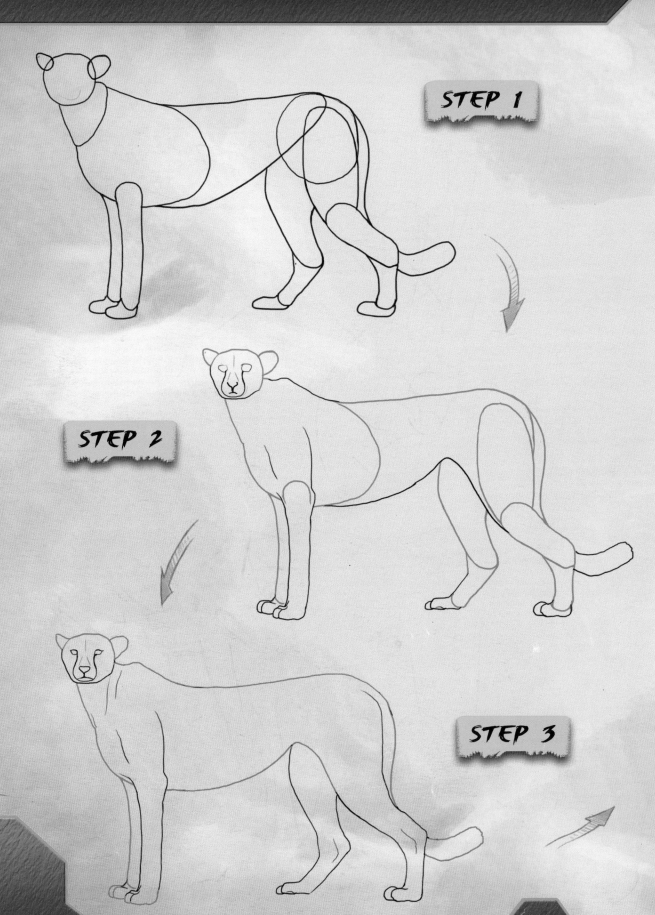

STEP 1

STEP 2

STEP 3

18

The cheetah holds the world's record for fastest land animal, capable of running up to 70 miles (113 kilometers) per hour. This big cat is built for speed, with a long spine and legs, and a large heart and lungs. But the cheetah's a sprinter, not a distance runner, and can only maintain top speed for a short time.

STEP 4

FINISHED!

CHIMPANZEE

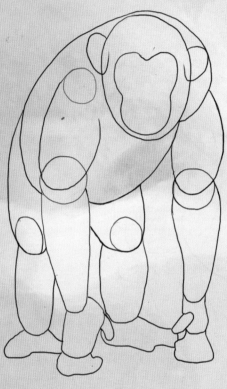

STEP 3

This African ape is human's closest relative. Chimps are social animals that live and hunt in groups, although they are mainly plant eaters. They are intelligent animals that communicate with one another using gestures, expressions, and many sounds. Chimps use tools, such as sticks to catch ants, and may even use plants as medicines.

STEP 4

FINISHED!

EASTERN DIAMONDBACK RATTLESNAKE

STEP 2

STEP 3

22

The famous rattling sound of a rattlesnake is its last warning before it strikes. The venom of the eastern diamondback can be deadly to humans, but most won't strike a human unless they're being bothered. This largest rattler in North America can grow to 8 feet (2.4 m) long and can strike at prey from about one-third that distance.

STEP 4

FINISHED!

EMPEROR PENGUIN

STEP 1

STEP 2

STEP 3

At 4 feet (1.2 m) tall, the emperor penguin is the largest penguin. It is also the deepest diver of any bird, diving to 600 yards (550 m) in search of fish and squid. Females lay one egg and leave it on their male partners' feet to incubate during the cold Antarctic winter. The females then head off on a 60-day fishing trip.

STEP 4

FINISHED!

STEP 1

STEP 2

STEP 3

Found only on the Galápagos Islands, these giant tortoises grow to a great size and live to an old age. They may reach 5 feet (1.5 m) or more in length and can weigh 550 pounds (250 kilograms). They may live longer than 100 years! These slow-moving plant eaters graze on grasses and cactus, but can survive for a year without eating.

STEP 4

FINISHED!

GIANT PANDA

STEP 1

STEP 2

STEP 3

These quiet, bamboo-munching mammals eat for 16 hours a day, because it takes a huge amount of bamboo to feed them. That means they also produce a lot of waste that they must get rid of—up to 50 times a day! Giant pandas use a thumblike part on their wrists to pick and feed themselves bamboo.

STEP 4

FINISHED!

GIRAFFE

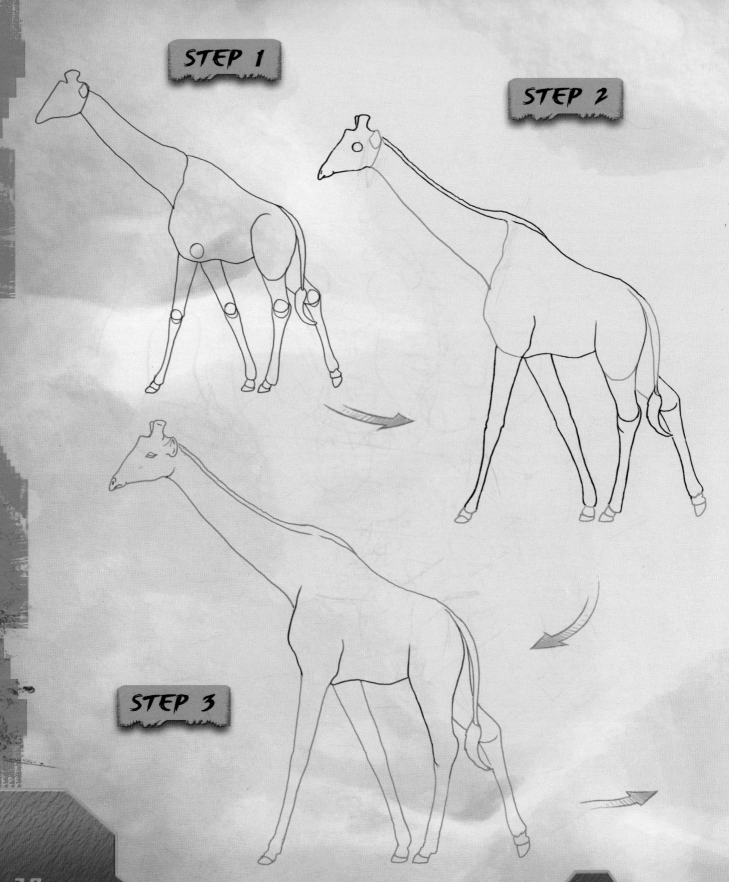

STEP 1

STEP 2

STEP 3

Every part of the giraffe is tall, from its legs to its neck to its tongue. These 14- to 19-foot (4.3- to 5.8-m) African mammals have legs up to 6 feet (1.8 m) long and tongues 21 inches (53 centimeters) long. These long features help the giraffe reach high into trees to eat leaves.

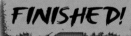

GRIZZLY BEAR

STEP 1

STEP 2

STEP 3

This species of brown bear is a 600-pound (272-kg) giant that eats nearly anything—fish, berries, nuts, roots, and animals, including moose. Named grizzly for the silvery, "grizzled" tips of its fur, this bear will fight to protect its young or its food. Grizzlies are also fast. They can run up to 30 miles (48 km) per hour.

STEP 4

FINISHED!

HARP SEAL

STEP 1

STEP 2

STEP 3

Baby harp seals are born with a furry white coat, but they shed it a few weeks after birth. Adult harp seals have sleek gray or white fur. They have dark markings on their backs in the shape of a harp, which is how they get their name. These social, ice-loving animals travel long distances each year to reach mating grounds.

STEP 4

FINISHED!

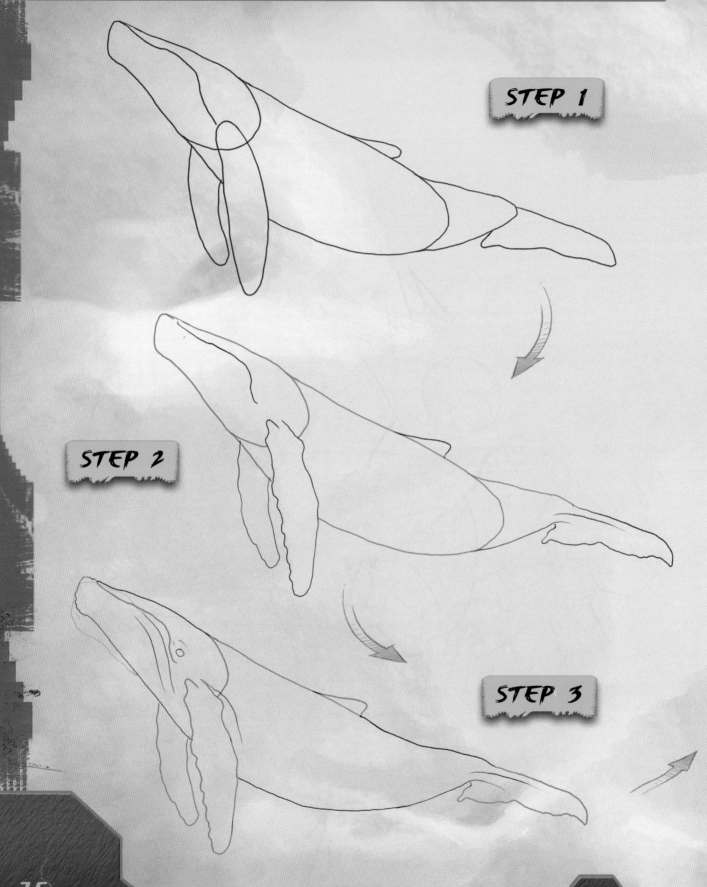

STEP 1

STEP 2

STEP 3

Humpbacks have long fins that they use to steer, brake, and defend themselves. These fins can be one-third the length of their 60-foot (18-m) bodies. Humpbacks are known for their moaning songs, which can be heard 20 miles (32 km) away. These giant mammals eat up to 3,000 pounds (1,360 kg) of food per day.

STEP 4

FINISHED!

KOALA

STEP 1

STEP 2

STEP 3

Koalas are Australian marsupials that feed on nearly 3 pounds (1.4 kg) of eucalyptus leaves daily. This diet doesn't provide many nutrients, which leaves koalas with little energy. A koala keeps its baby in a pouch. After several months, the joey crawls up onto its mother's back and stays there until it's about a year old.

FINISHED!

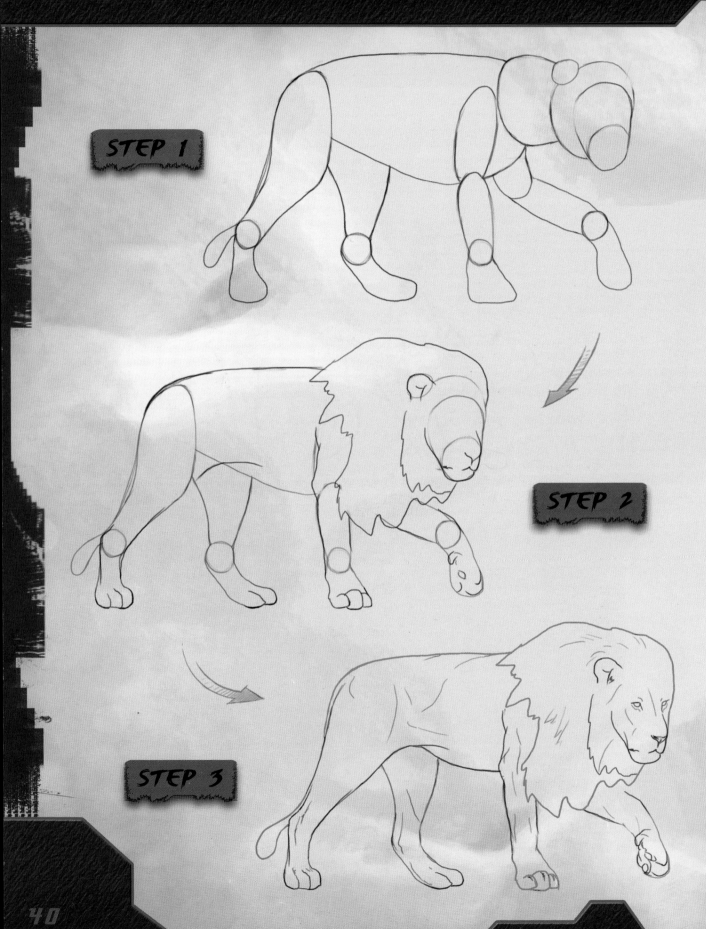

STEP 1

STEP 2

STEP 3

Lions live on the African savannas in groups called prides, which include about 15 lions. Prides have many females, one or two males, and young cubs. The females work together to hunt zebras, antelopes, and even hippos. Males defend the pride. They often fight other males over leadership of their prides.

STEP 4

FINISHED!

MEERKAT

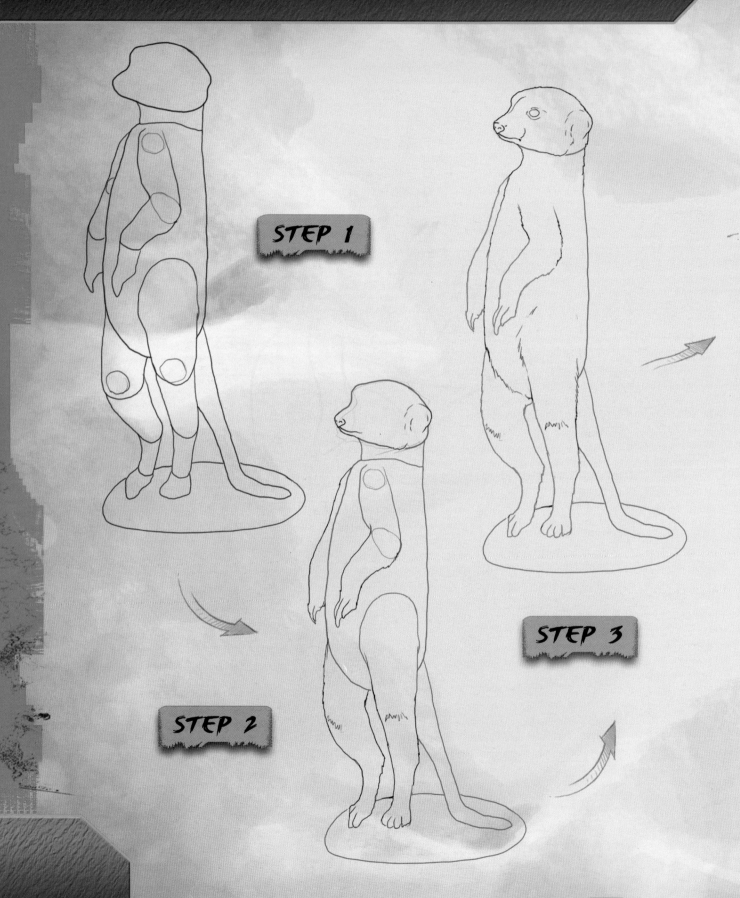

STEP 1

STEP 2

STEP 3

When a meerkat is in its standing position, it's looking out for predators—typically jackals or raptors. Meerkats spend their nights in underground tunnels. During the day they hunt nearby for beetles, spiders, lizards, and small rodents. Sometimes one meerkat will stand guard while the others hunt, sending out a warning call if it sees a predator.

STEP 4

FINISHED!

MONARCH BUTTERFLY

STEP 1

STEP 2

STEP 3

This large butterfly is a common sight throughout North and South America. It makes an 1,800-mile (2,900-km) winter migration to California or Mexico. Monarchs lay their eggs during the return trip in spring. Adults live only three to four weeks, so their offspring must continue the trip for them.

STEP 4

FINISHED!

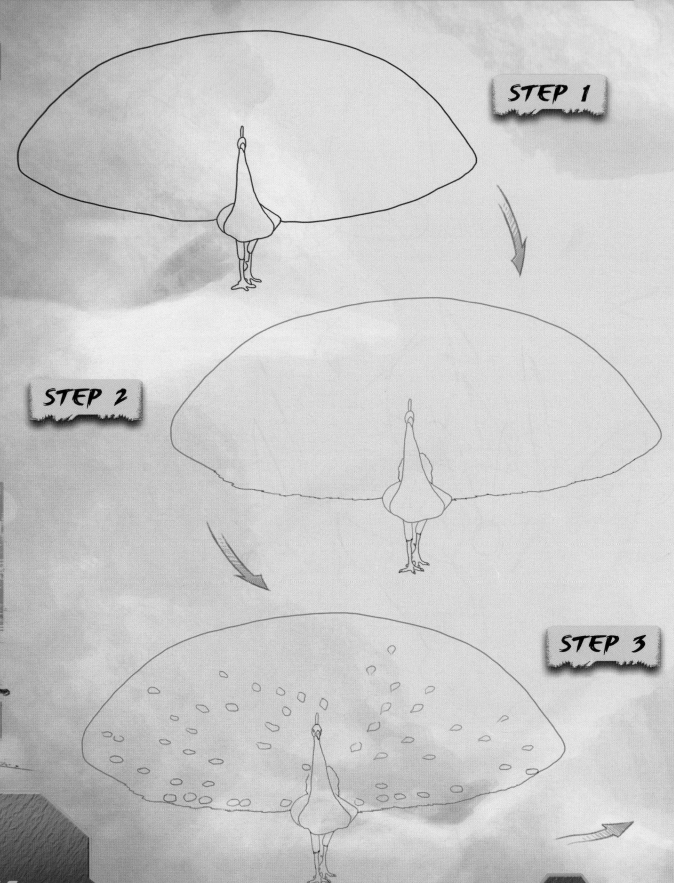

STEP 1

STEP 2

STEP 3

Peacocks, also called peafowl, are beautiful blue-green birds with a large spray of feathers on their tails. But only the males have these feathers, which they fan out and display to females. The females, called peahens, are less colorful. Peacocks are turkey-sized birds that belong to the pheasant family and live in warm climates.

STEP 4

FINISHED!

PLATYPUS

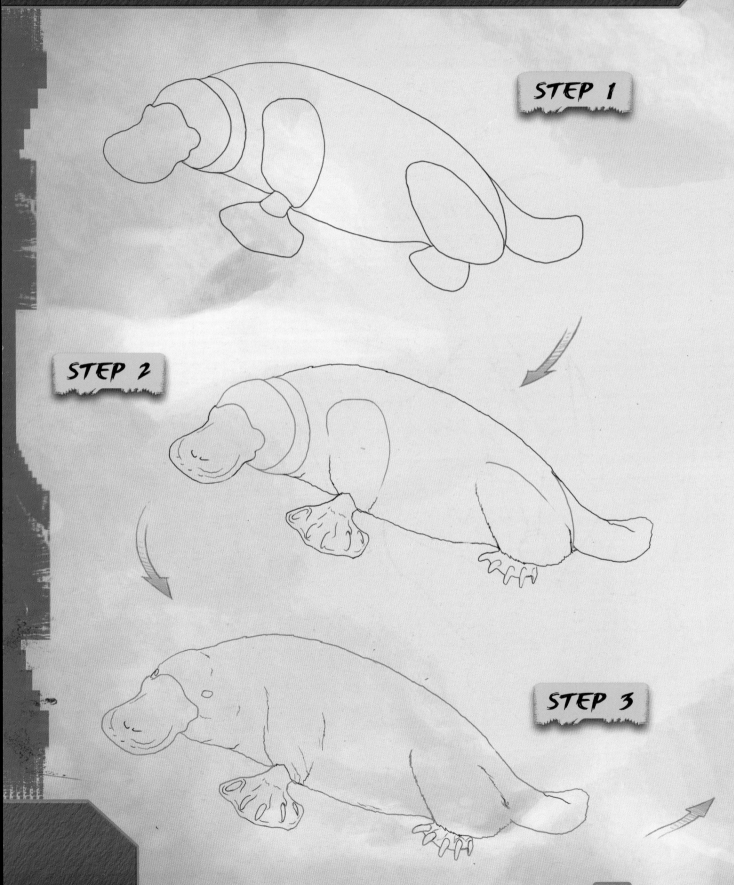

STEP 1

STEP 2

STEP 3

This Australian mammal, also called a duckbill, is perfectly built for the water. It has a streamlined body for fast swimming, and thick, waterproof fur. Its unusual bill allows it to shovel through dirt and plants to find insects, frogs, and crustaceans to eat.

STEP 4

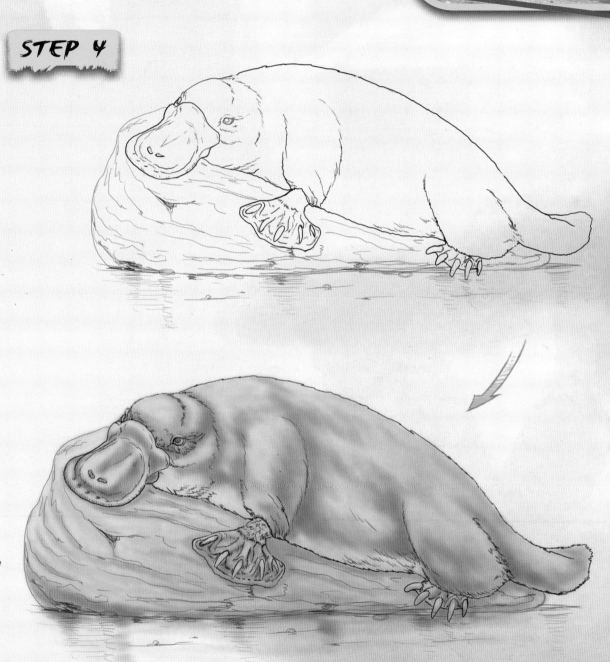

FINISHED!

POISON DART FROG

The skin of poison dart frogs contains a poison, which the frogs use to fend off predators. The poison of a few species can be deadly to humans. Some people of the Amazon rain forest put the poison of these frogs on the tips of darts. They use the poison darts to hunt animals.

STEP 4

FINISHED!

PORCUPINE

STEP 1

STEP 2

STEP 3

The quills of a porcupine are long, sharp hairs that grow together to make pointy bristles. The quills are usually pointed down, but the porcupine will raise them in defense when threatened. If an enemy gets too close, the quills have jagged barbs that work like fishhooks to painfully stick in the predator's skin.

STEP 4

FINISHED!

RED KANGAROO

STEP 1

STEP 2

STEP 3

Red kangaroos have powerful hind legs that always move together. They can travel up to 25 feet (7.6 m) in one jump. They can also lean back on their strong tails and kick their feet at enemies. Baby joeys are the size of a lima bean at birth and stay in their mothers' pouches on and off until about 8 months of age.

STEP 4

FINISHED!

TARANTULA

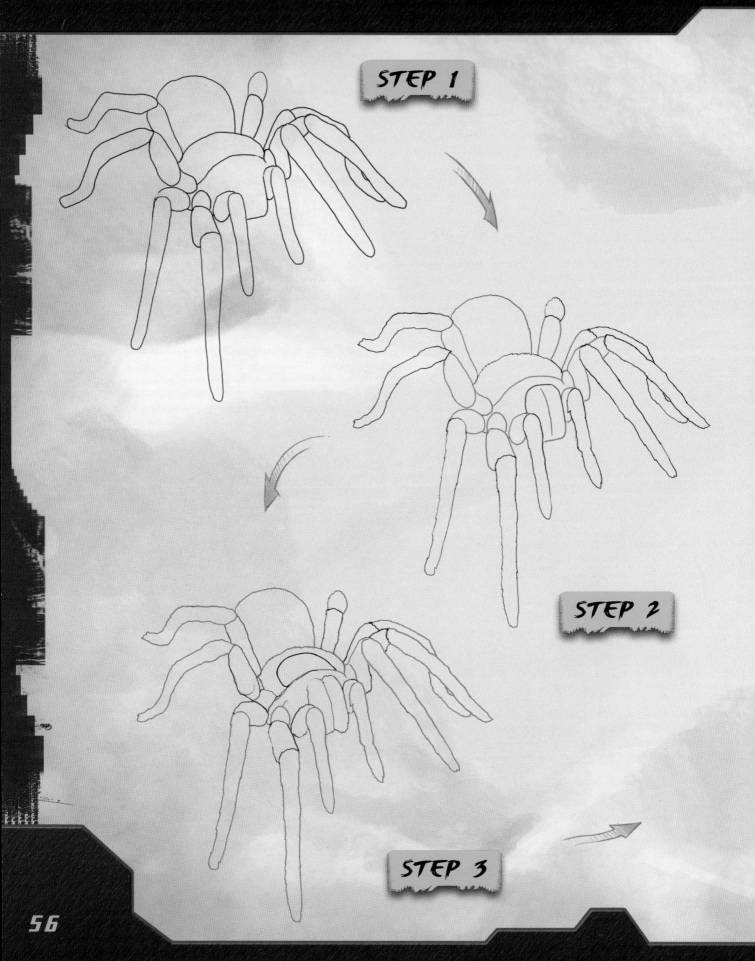

STEP 1

STEP 2

STEP 3

Tarantulas are large, hairy spiders that are popular as pets. Tarantulas catch their prey by chasing it instead of using a web. They hunt insects, small toads, and mice. These spiders can be 2 inches (5 cm) long with a leg span of almost 5 inches (13 cm). Their bite can be painful to humans, but it's not dangerous.

STEP 4

FINISHED!

VAMPIRE BAT

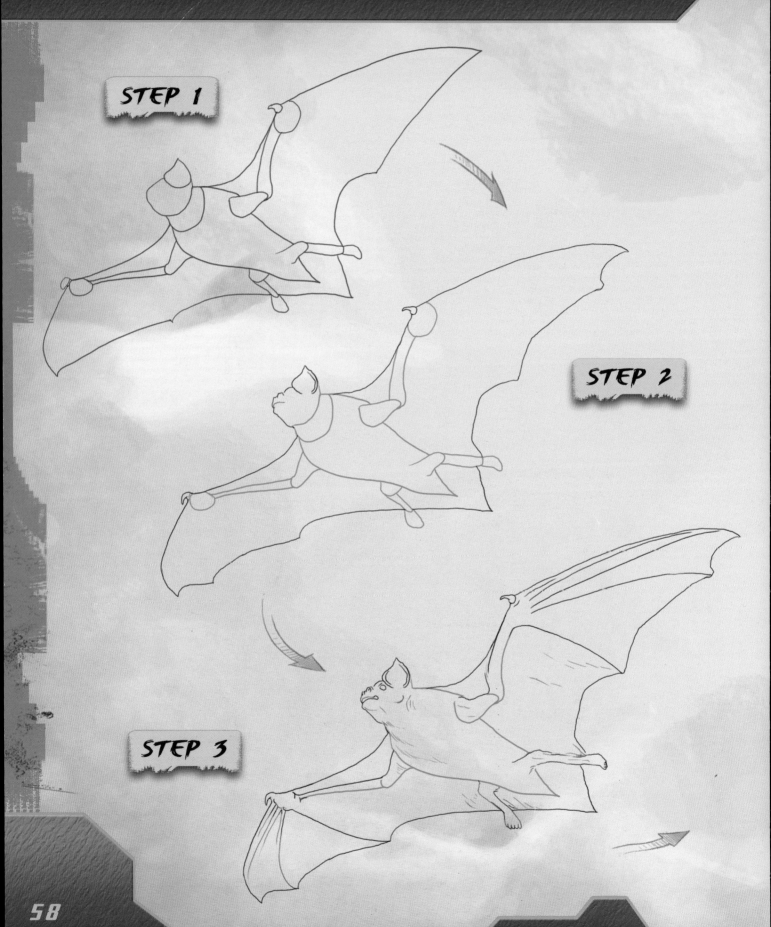

Vampire bats got their gory name because they feed on blood—typically the blood of farm and forest animals. A 2-ounce (57-gram) bat can double its body weight after a blood meal. Like other bats, vampire bats use echolocation to find their prey during nightly hunts. They use heat sensors on their faces to detect warmth from prey animals.

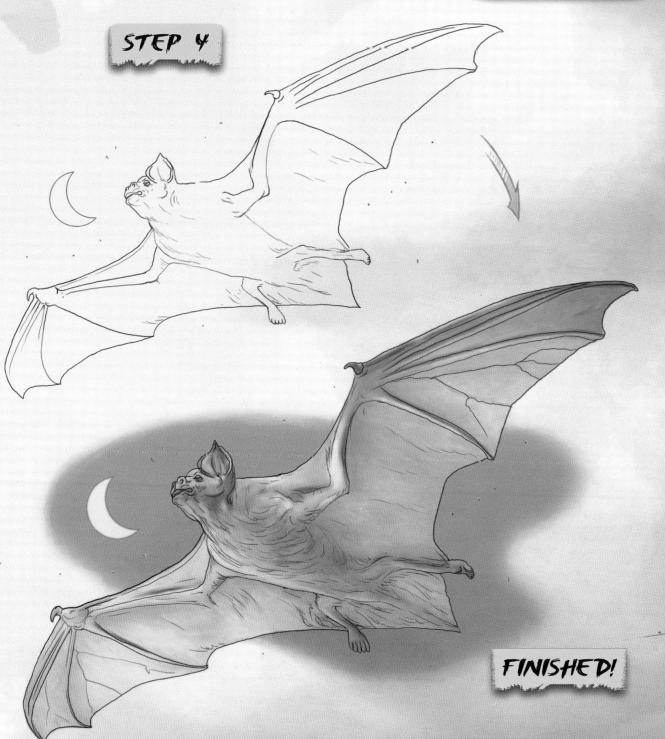

STEP 4

FINISHED!

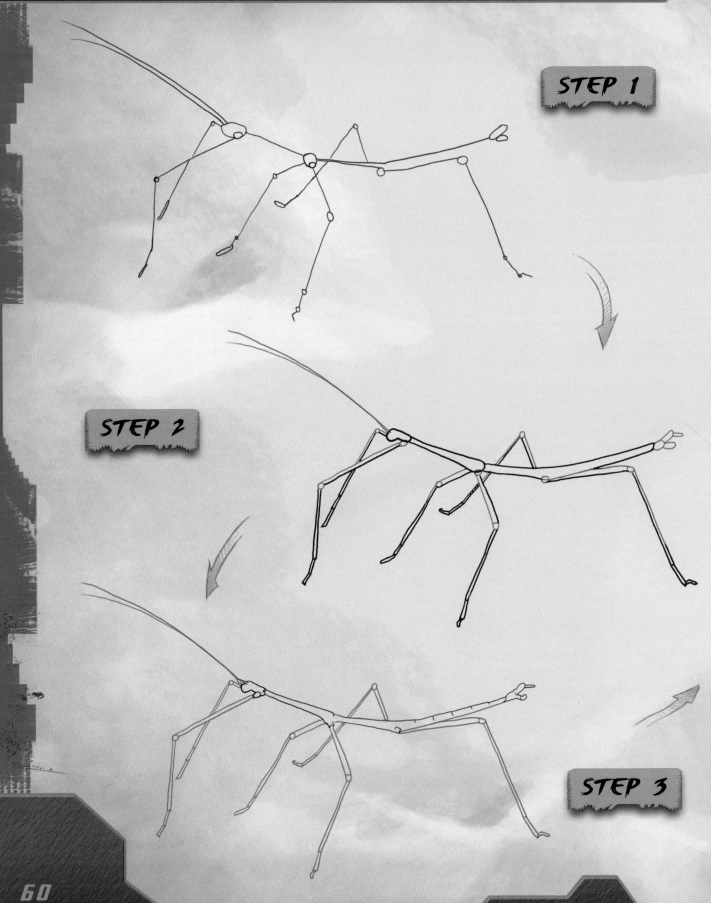

STEP 1

STEP 2

STEP 3

Walking sticks, also called stick insects, are excellent hiders. Their bodies look like the twigs of trees. Like sticks, they don't move much. Stick insects sit still, nibbling on leaves and hiding from predators. They even have a way to camouflage their offspring—the eggs of some species look like seeds.

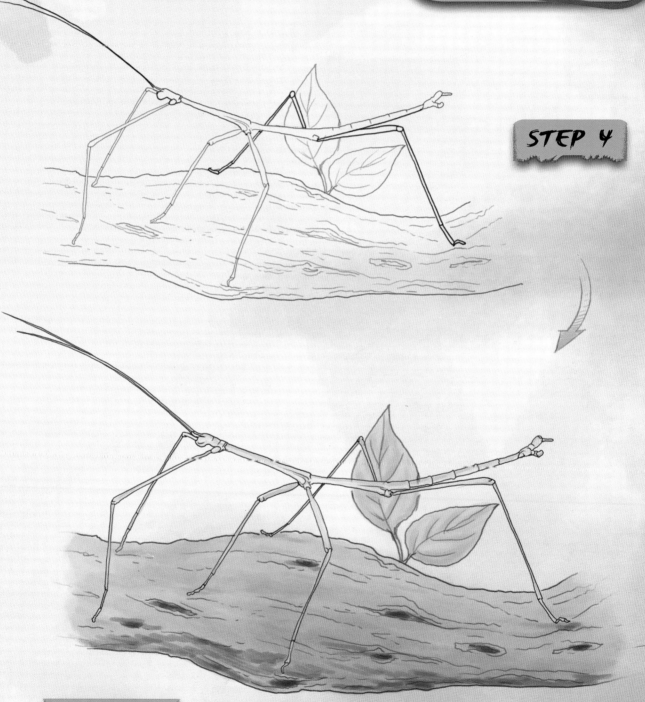

STEP 4

FINISHED!

STEP 1

STEP 2

STEP 3

Wolverines are short, stout members of the weasel family that look like small bears with tails. For their small size, they are strong, fierce hunters. They attack rodents, sheep, deer, and even caribou in their northern and tundra habitats. If desperate for food, a wolverine may dig into the burrows of hibernating animals and eat them.

STEP 4

FINISHED!

Capstone Press
1710 Roe Crest Drive
North Mankato, Minnesota 56003
www.capstonepub.com

Library of Congress Cataloging-in-Publication Data
McCurry, Kristen.
  How to draw amazing animals / by Kristen McCurry ; illustrations by Leonardo Meschini.
    pages cm. — (Smithsonian drawing books)
  Summary: "Provides information and step-by-step drawing instructions for 30 popular animals"—Provided by publisher.
  ISBN 978-1-4296-9939-6 (library binding)
  ISBN 978-1-62065-726-3 (paperback)
1. Animals in art—Juvenile literature. 2. Drawing—Technique—Juvenile literature. I. Meschini, Leonardo, 1973– illustrator. II. Title.
NC780.M39 2013
  743.6—dc23   2012031830

Editorial Credits:
Kristen Mohn, editor
Alison Thiele, designer
Nathan Gassman, art director
Eric Gohl, media researcher
Laura Manthe, production specialist

Our very special thanks to Don E. Wilson, PhD, Curator Emeritus of the Department of Vertebrate Zoology at the Smithsonian's National Museum of Natural History for his curatorial review. Capstone would also like to thank Ellen Nanney and Kealy Wilson at the Smithsonian Institution's Office of Licensing for their help in the creation of this book.

Smithsonian Enterprises: Carol LeBlanc, Vice President; Brigid Ferraro, Director of Licensing

Photo credits:
BigStockPhoto.com: desertrosestudios, 37; Fotolia: Fabrice Beauchene, 25, Kitch Bain, 21; iStockphotos: John Carnemolla, 49; Shutterstock: Abramova Kseniya, 9, Audrey Snider-Bell, 57, Bridgena Barnard, 19, Daniel Alvarez, 27, Dennis Donohue, 41, Eduard Kyslynskyy, 55, Gerrit de Vries, 17, Heiko Kiera, 23, Hung Chung Chih, 29, James Laurie, 45, Johan W. Elzenga, 5, Johan Larson, 61, John Arnold, 51, Mammut Vision, 7, Michael Lynch, 59, mlorenz, 13, mooinblack, 43, Mykhaylo Palinchak, 47, Peter Wey, 11, Pichugin Dmitry, 31, Pyshnyy Maxim Vjacheslavovich, 15, Scott E Read, 33, tratong, 53, Vladimir Melnik, 35, worldswildlifewonders, 39; Wikipedia: National Park Service, 63

INTERNET SITES

FactHound offers a safe, fun way to find Internet sites related to this book. All sites on FactHound have been researched by our staff.

Here's all you do:

Visit www.facthound.com

Type in this code: 9781429699396

Super-cool stuff! Check out projects, games and lots more at **www.capstonekids.com**

Printed in the United States of America in North Mankato Minnesota.
092012   006933CGS13